PRE-SCHOOL FOLLOWING DIRECTIONS

Fun-filled Activities

An imprint of Om Books International

The [mouse] is UP.

Tick (✓) the one who is UP.

Draw a  ∼ from the [hand] to [carrot].

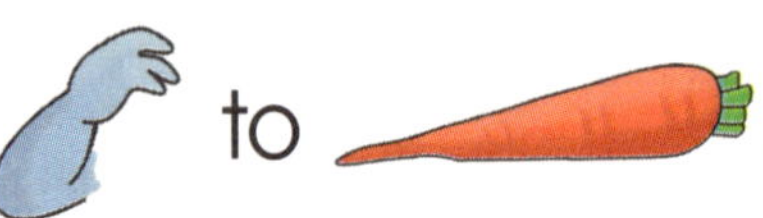

Down

The is DOWN.

Draw a ◯ around the one who is DOWN.

Colour the  green.

On

The  is ON the .

What is ON the head of the  ? Tick (✓).

Trace the dotted lines to complete the picture.

The  is IN the .

Draw a  ◯ around the one who is IN.

Draw a  near the .

Top

The  is on the TOP.

Tick (✓) the one who is on the TOP.

Draw 3  s in the basket.

Bottom

The  is at the BOTTOM.

Draw a  ◯ around the head of the one who is at the BOTTOM.

Trace the ball and colour it.

Under

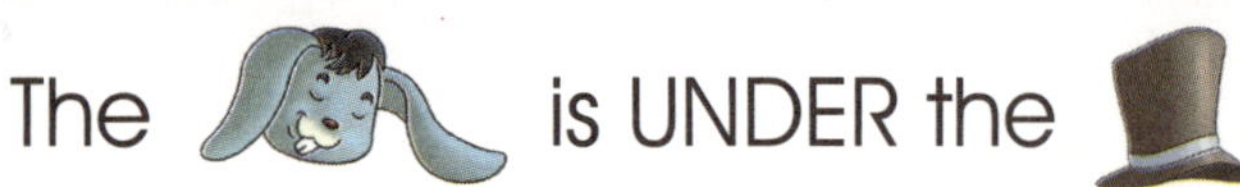

The is UNDER the .

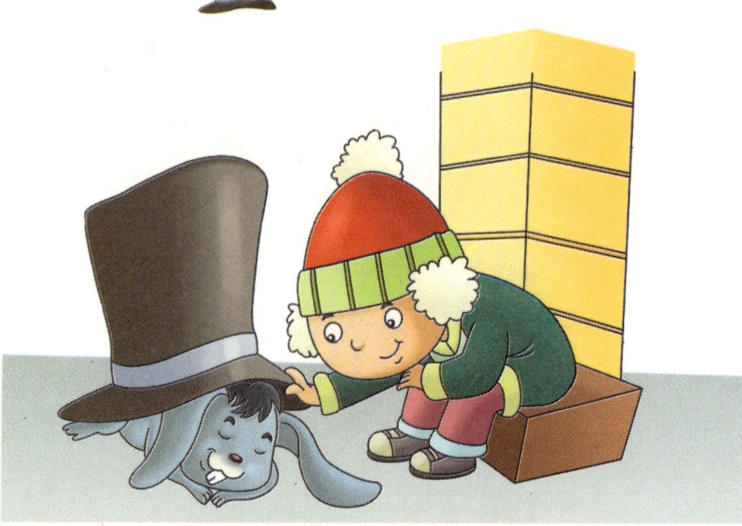

Tick (√) the one who is UNDER.

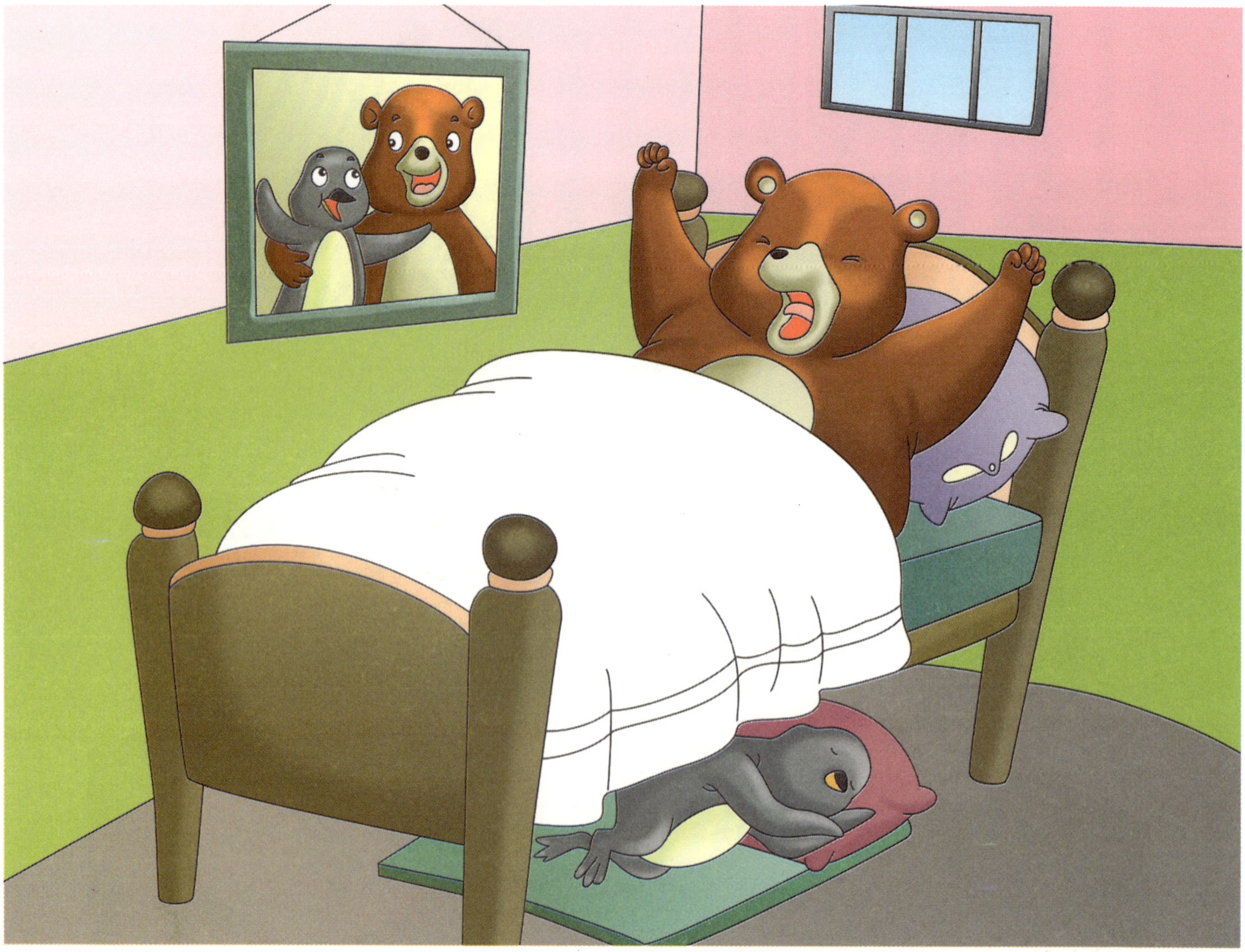

Colour the 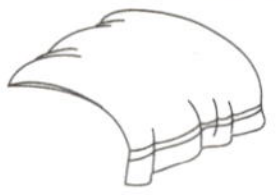 pink.

The is on the LEFT of .

Draw a ◯ around the one who is to the LEFT of the  .

Draw a △ on the  .

The  is to the RIGHT of the  .

Tick (✓) the one who is to the RIGHT of  .

Draw a  on the and colour it.

Draw 4 ◯s on the ⛄.

Draw an X on the one who is to the RIGHT of the .

Colour the kites  .

Draw a  from the 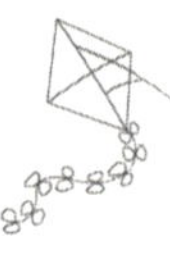 to the .

Draw a 🔴 in the 🧤.

Tick (✓) what is ON the head of the  .

Draw and Colour

Draw the  s of the  .

Colour the  .

Draw 3  s on the  .

Draw a  ◯ around what is IN the  .

Trace over the dotted lines and complete the picture.

Colour the   with s.

Draw and Colour

Draw 3 s above Tinny's LEFT .

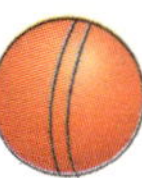

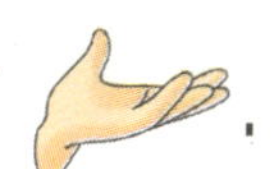

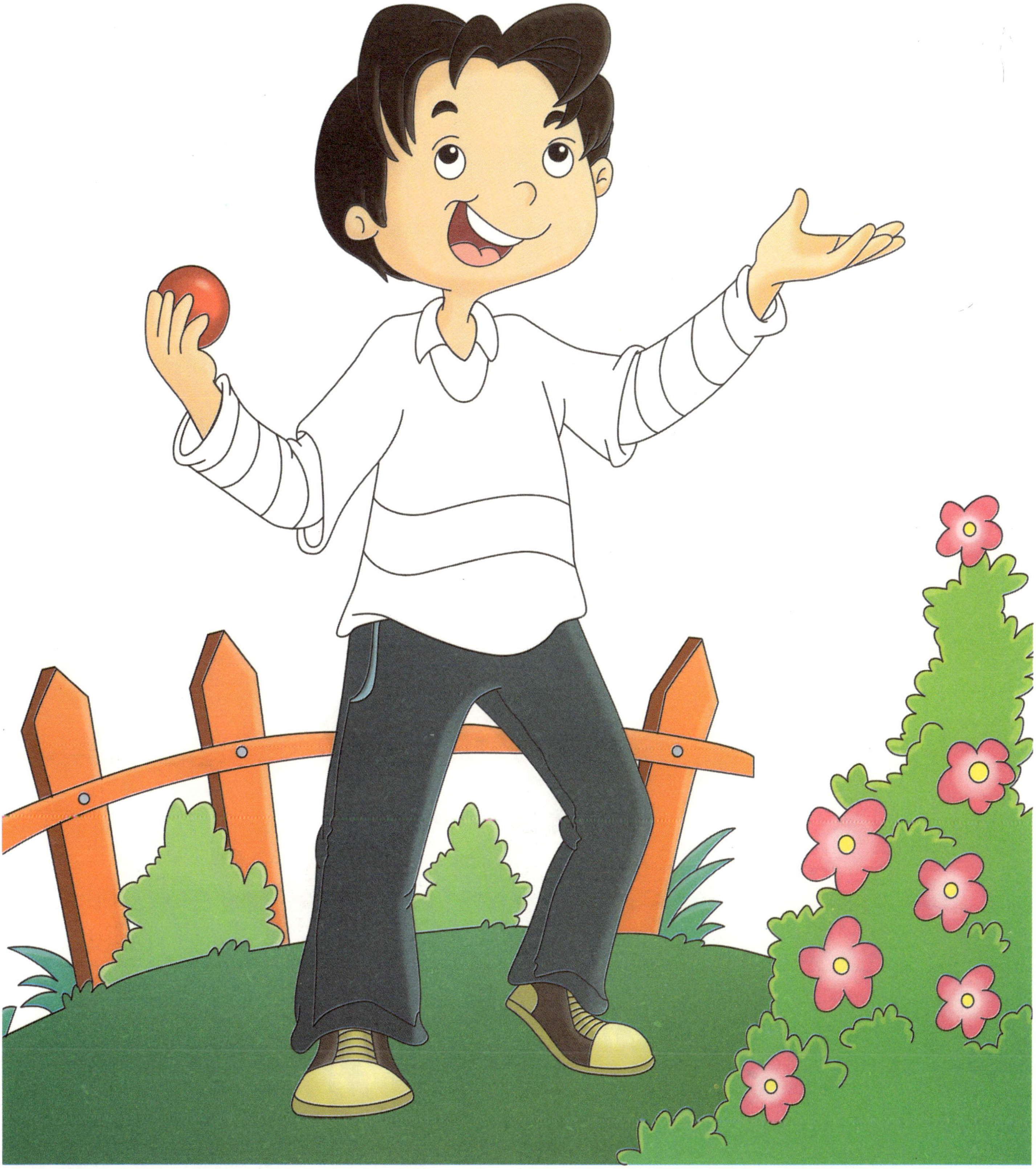

Colour the with s.

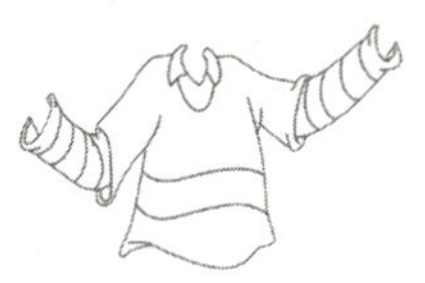

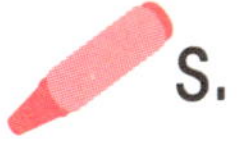

Draw s around the .

Colour the   .

Draw a △ around the 🥛s.

Draw 3  ON the .

Draw ◯ around the  and complete the picture.

Draw a ☐ around the one who is UNDER the .

Join the dots from N to P and complete the picture.

Write 8 in the ⬯ and colour the .

Draw ═══ on the ⌂.

Draw a ◯ around the one who is DOWN.

Draw and Colour

Draw 6 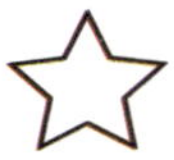 on the 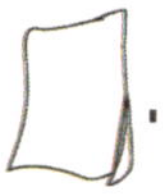.

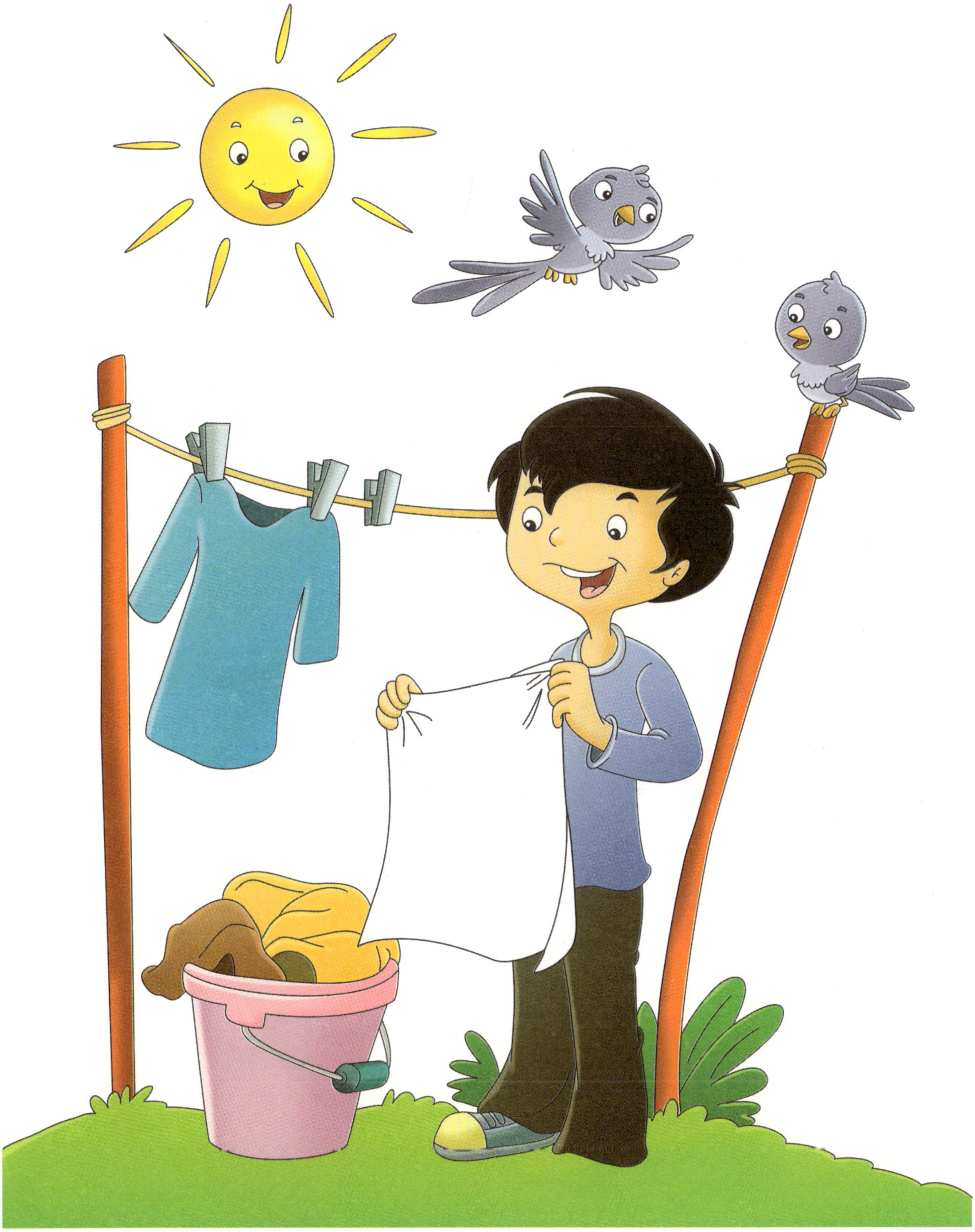

Draw the missing . Colour it.

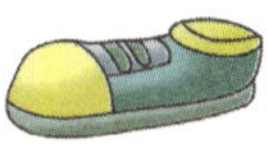

Read and Do

Draw an X on all 6s in the picture.

Colour the  with a .

Draw a  around the  with  .

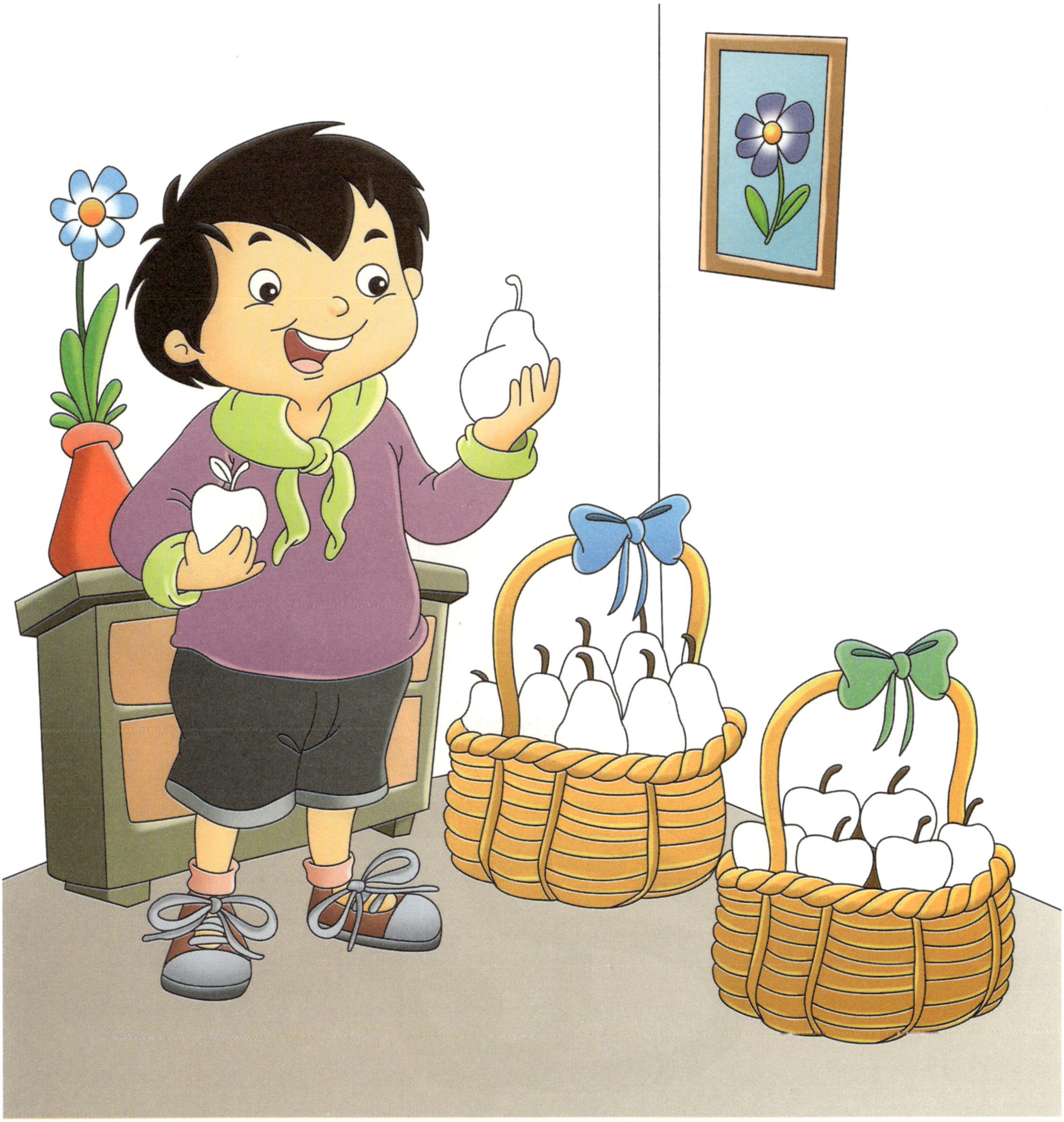

Colour the  and the  .

Draw 〜 from START to help the hen find 3 eggs.

Draw a ☐ around 4 eggs.

Tick (√) the that is on the TOP.

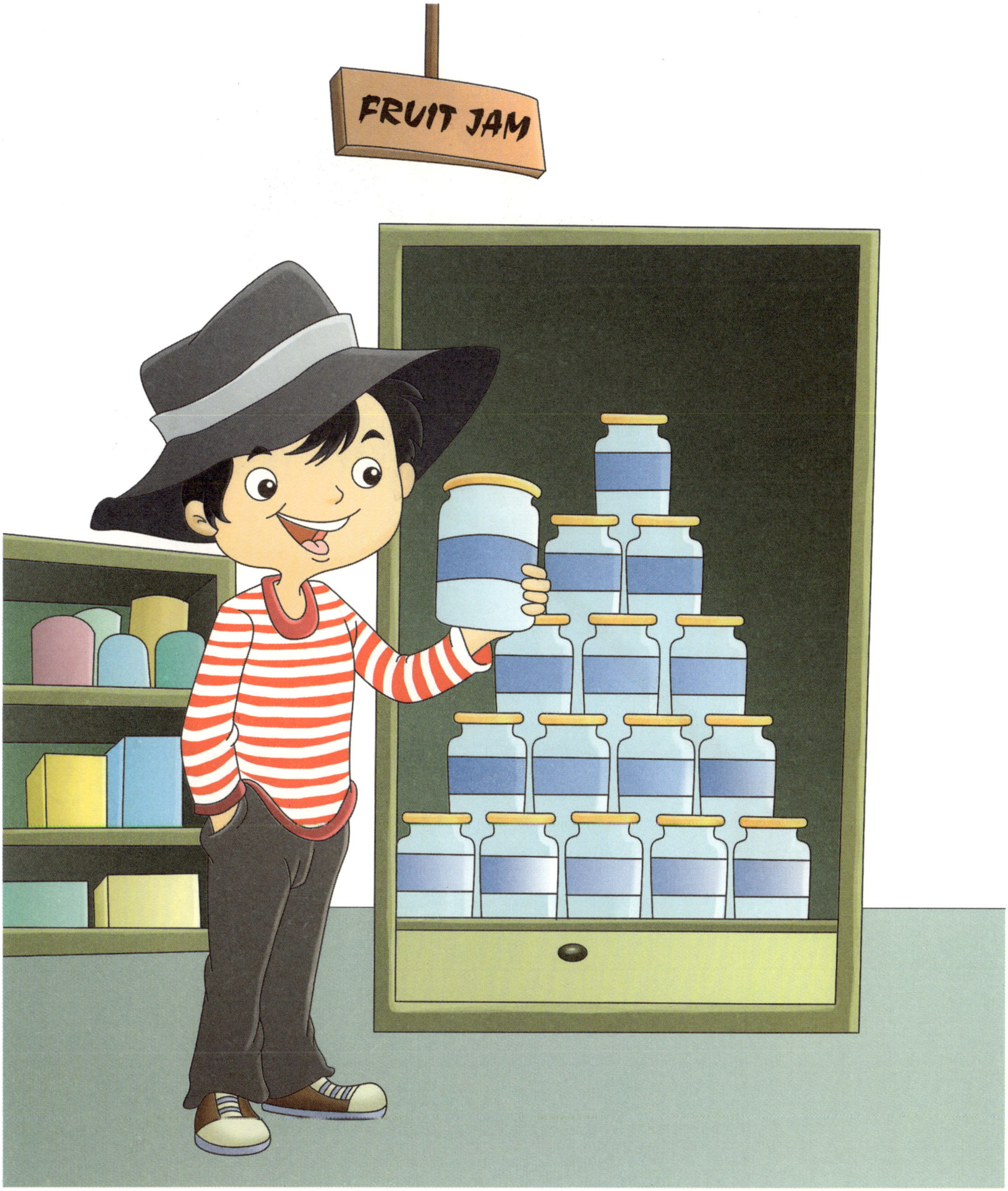

Draw an X on the s that are at the BOTTOM.

Join the dots from 1 to 10 and complete the picture.

Draw 2  in water.

Follow the number key to colour the picture.

Draw a ON the .

Draw 3 in the girl's

on the .

A to the LEFT of the .

A UP near the .

Colour the .